Tried and True
ESL Lessons

Level 1
Book A

Student

Barbara Kinney Black

DEDICATION

A dedication can only be to my Lord Jesus Christ who is the 'author and finisher of our faith' and the One who directed the writing of this volume.

CONTENTS

ACKNOWLEDGMENTS

Special thanks to my husband for his unending patient assistance, his photographic skill, and attention to detail in the editing process. Also for assuming numerous tasks during the writing process.
Heartfelt thanks also to the 'praying ladies' of Pines Baptist Church who provided much needed constant prayer support.

Hello Students!

Welcome to Tried and True ESL Lessons. You're about to begin a journey of discovery and excitement while learning the world' most popular language English.

Work hard, speak every day, and you'll soon be on your way to new adventures in the world of the English language. There's a lot of people cheering for you as you begin this journey, and know that you have already been prayed for.

Sincerely,
Your instructor,
Professor Black

UNIT 1
PERSONAL COMMUNICATION
LESSON 1 – INTRODUCTIONS

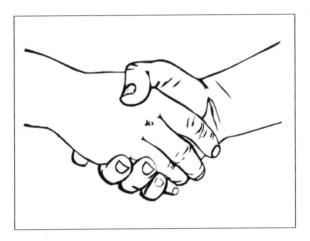

shake hands

M-A-R-I-A

spell

Registration

Name: Barbara

Country Cuba

registration form

HELLO,
my name is:
Barbara

name

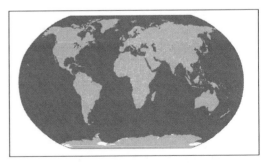

country from

To Do First: Repeat the conversation after the instructor.

What's Your Name?
Speaker A: New Student   Speaker B: Instructor

1.A.   Hi. I want to register for class.
   1.B.   O.K. What's your name?
2.A.   My name is **Juan Roque**.
   2.B.   How do you spell that?
3.A.   **J-U-A-N   R-O-Q-U-E**.
   3.B.   Where are you from?
4.A.   I'm from **Venezuela**.
   4.B.   Nice to meet you.

To Do Second: Speak with a partner. Change the underlined words in the conversation for the Substitutions in No. 1-3 below.

Substitution No. 1

2.A.   My name is Rosangela Morado.
3.A.   R-O-S-A-N-G-E-L-A   M-O-R-A-D-O.
4.A.   I'm from Brazil.

Substitution No. 2

2.A.   My name is Ming Lee.
3.A.   M-I-N-G   L-E-E.
4.A.   I'm from China.

Substitution No. 3

2.A.   My name is Fredeline Francois.
3.A.   F-R-E-D-E-L-I-N-E   F-R-A-N-C-O-I-S.
4.A.   I'm from Haiti.

Grammar Foundation

To Do First:
Repeat each sentence after the instructor.

1. To Be Verb

The Be Verb is used to describe State of Being. We use it to describe (1) how we are, or (2) who we are, or (3) a place we are at. For example:

How we are:	Who we are	Where we are:
I am sick.	I am a teacher.	I am at the library.
You are happy.	You are a student.	You are at McDonalds.
She is hungry.	She is a mother.	She is at work.

Statements

Subject + Be Verb			Subject + Be Verb		
Singular Forms			**Plural Forms**		
I	am	a teacher.	We	are	tired.
You	are	a student.	We	are	friends.
He	is	well.	You	are	in Chicago.
He	is	an uncle.	They	are	absent.
She	is	at church.	They	are	sisters.
It	is	raining.			

To Do Second:
Speak to a partner. Make statements about yourself, your family, and other students.

To Do Third:
Repeat each question and answer after the instructor.

2. Asking WH-Questions

WH-Questions are questions which begin with a question word: who, what, where, when, why, or how. The answer gives specific information.

Question Word	The Answer is About
Who	a person
What	a thing

Where	a place
When	time
Why	the reason
How	the process

WH-Question + Be Verb			Answers
Singular Forms			
What	is	your name?	My name is Barbara.
What	is	your address?	My address is 2110 N.W. 152 Street.
Who	is	he?	He is my brother.
Where	is	she?	She is at school.
Who	is	your friend?	His name is Rolando.
When	is	your class?	It's at 7:00.
How old	are	you?	I'm 25 years old.
Where	are	you from?	I'm from Haiti.
Plural Forms			
What		are those flowers?	They are roses.
Who		are those people?	They are new students.
Where		are those students from?	They are from China.
When		are John and Jerry coming back?	They are coming back in January.

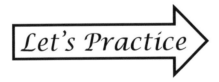

Let's Practice

1. How Do You Spell That?

To Do:

1. Speak with a partner. Use the Conversation and Substitutions. Practice spelling the names.
2. Write your name on the board with large letters.
3. The instructor will ask students to spell names.

2. Where Are You From?

To Do:

1. Write your name on a small paper.
2. The instructor will ask you, "Where are you from?" Answer the question, for example, "I'm from Cuba."

3. Put your name on the map by your country.
4. Spell the country names.

3. Interview Line-Up
To Do:
1. Follow the instructor's directions. Make a line with other students.
2. Ask questions to other students. The instructor will give you the questions.

4. Play Beat the Cat
1. This game is like the TV show Wheel of Fortune. The instructor will put a puzzle on the board.
2. Students take turns guessing consonants.
3. If the consonant is in the puzzle, the instructor will write it on the line. If the consonant is NOT in the puzzle, the instructor will draw part of a cat.
4. Continue until only vowels are left in the puzzle.

Review Exercises

1. Complete the Questions – Answer the Questions

To Do:

1. Complete the questions.
2. Answer the questions.

Questions	Answers
1. What's *your name?*	*My name*
2. Where	

2. Correct the Mistakes

To Do:

1. The sentences under Wrong Sentence are incorrect. Find the mistake.
2. Write the Correct Sentence.

Wrong Sentence	Correct Sentence
1. What your name?	*What's your name.*
2. What are you from?	
3. Where the instructor from?	
4. I'm from Spanish.	
5. My name is Brazil.	
6. The instructor's name is Haiti.	

3. Circle the Hidden Words

To Do:

Circle the words in the puzzle.

name   speak   spell   language   class   welcome

```
A  S  D  F  G  H  [N  A  M  E]  K  L  I  Y  N  M  E  N  W  Q  N  B  B  Y  U  N  E  A

N  Y  U  I  Y  T  E  N  W  E  T  N  B  G  Y  N  E  W  T  L  A  N  G  U  A  G  E  U

G  U  Y  N  M  I  N  C  L  A  S  S  Y  I  O  Y  B  A  S  D  B  N  Y  I  Y  T  Q  X

S  P  E  L  L  H  N  Y  I  O  P  Y  B  V  C  X  Z  S  E  W  Q  N  I  Y  I  O  P  N

W  N  I  O  H  N  I  O  P  U  U  W  Q  W  E  W  E  L  C  O  M  E  Y  N  R  I  O  W

Y  U  T  I  O  P  Y  E  R  B  Q  U  N  I  O  B  M  B  E  V  C  O  S  P  E  A  K  G
```

4. Introduce Yourself

To Do:

1. Introduce yourself to 3 people this week. Tell your name and where you are from.
2. Ask their name and where they are from.
3. Tell the class about it next week.

5. Use the Grammar

To Do:

Complete the sentences with the correct form of the BE Verb.

1. What __is__ your name?

2. Where _____ you from?

3. When _____ your interview?

4. We _____ hungry.

5. They _____ absent.

6. My son _____ at the library.

7. Where _____ your friends from?

8. What time _____ it?

9. It _____ not raining.

10. They _____ not in class.

Keep up the good work!

UNIT 1
PERSONAL COMMUNICATION
LESSON 2 – THE FAMILY

MARIA'S FAMILY TREE

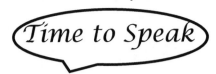

Time to Speak

To Do First: Repeat the conversation after the instructor.

This is My Family

1.A.   This is a picture of my family.

  1.B.   Who's that?

2.A.   That's my father, Michael.

  2.B.   And who is she?

3.A.   She is my mother, Monica.

  3.B.   Who is he?

4.A.   He is my husband, Henry.

  4.B.   And who are they?

5.A.   They are my children, Paula and Peter.

To Do Second:

  1. Practice the conversation with a partner.
  2. Volunteer pairs present their conversations for the class.

To Do Third:

  1. Draw a picture of your family or show a picture on your cell phone. Work with a partner.
  2. Student 2 asks Student 1, "Who is that?" while pointing to one of the family members in Student 1's picture. Student 1 answers, for example: "She is my daughter."
  3. Continue until Student 1 has identified all family members.
  4. Repeat the activity with Student 2's family picture.

Grammar Foundation

1. Asking Questions with WHO
The question word WHO is used to ask about a person. For example:

Who + Be + Object   Answers

Singular Forms

Who	are	you?	I am Mrs. Black
Who	is	he?	He is my father.
Who	is	she?	She is my mother.
Who	is	Mrs. Black?	She is my sister.
Who	is	your teacher?	Mrs. Black is my teacher.
Who	is	that?	That is my husband.

Plural Forms

| Who | are | you? | We are your students. |
| Who | are | they? | They are my children. |

2. Using the Verb To BE
Use BE to talk about who a person is.

To Do First: Repeat each example sentence after the instructor.

Subject + Be

Singular Forms

I	am	a woman.
You	are	a student.
He	is	my father.
She	is	my wife.
Maria	is	my sister.
John	is	my husband.
Kiki	is	my cat.

Plural Forms

We	are	your students.
You	are	my friends.
They	are	my children.

Grammar is the foundation for learning language. Build well.

To Do Second: Students make sentences about their own family.

3. Subject Pronouns

We use SUBJECT PRONOUNS to take the place of a Subject in a sentence. The first time you talk about a person, use the person's name, for example: This is Maria. The second time you can use the Subject Pronoun, for example: 'She is my friend.'

To Do: Repeat each Subject Pronoun after the instructor.

Singular Forms	**Plural Forms**
I	we
you	you
he	they
she	
it	

~~ *Practicing Perfect Pronunciation* ~~

1. Practicing the Sounds of /t/ and /th/

The sounds of /t/ as in sister and daughter, and the sound of /th/ as in mother, father, and brother, are said very differently.

To pronounce the /t/ sound, place the tip of the tongue behind the front teeth. Blow out air to pronounce. Let the air push your tongue down.

To Do: Repeat after the instructor:
sister   daughter

To produce the /th/ sound, place the tip of the tongue between the teeth and begin to pronounce the /th/ sound. Bring the tongue back into the mouth to finish the sound. You can use a mirror to help see where your tongue is.

To Do: Repeat after the instructor:
mother   father   brother

2. Practicing the /z/ Sound in Contractions

English speakers use contractions—two words put together. Here's some contractions.

Full Form	Contraction
who is	who's
she is	she's
he is	he's

To pronounce the 's on the Contraction, make a /z/ sound. Make the /z/ sound just like the /s/ sound, but vibrate your voice box. Place your hands on your throat (neck) and feel your voice box. When you make the /z/ sound, your voice box will buzz like a bee. This is called vibration.

To Do: Practice with the instructor.

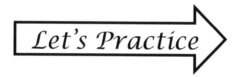
Let's Practice

1. Dictation
1. The instructor will write the family words on the board.
2. The instructor will spell a family word. Write the letters on your paper.
3. Find the family word on the board. Write the number of the word next to the word you spelled.
4. Check your answers with the class.

2. Male/Female Family Words – Categorizing
1. The instructor will say a family word, for example: "mother." The instructor will throw a ball to Student 1.
2. Student 1 catches the ball and says the opposite of mother, for example: "father."
3. Student 1 throws the ball to the instructor.

3. Family Pictures – Listening Activity
1. Open your book to the Family Pictures Listening Activity page.
2. You will hear some conversations. Circle the word in the [brackets] that you hear.
3. The instructor will play the conversation as many times as students ask.

1.A.   [Who's / Who] that?

  1.B.   [That / That's] my mother, Melinda.

2.A.   And who is [she / he]?

  2.B.   [He / She] is my sister, Moeisha.

3.A.   Who are they?

  3.B.   They [is / are] my three [children / childs] Peter, Paul, and Patrick.

4.A.   Who [is / are] they?

  4.B.   They are my [brothers / mothers]. His name is [John / Tom] and [his / hers] name is Tom.

5.A.   Who is he?

  5.B.   [He / She] is my husband, Bernie.

6.A.   [You / Do] have a nice family.

  6.B.   Thank you.

3. Verse Picture Puzzle

There are 6 pictures below. They tell a story. Look at and read the pictures.
Number them into correct order. Read for the class.

His love

God's children

_____
_____
_____

_____
_____
_____

the Father

is SO great that we are called

_____
_____
_____

_____
_____
_____

has ♡ us.

how much

_____
_____
_____

_____
_____
_____

Review Exercises

1. Put the Family Words into Alphabetical (A-Z) Order

A. mother   B. father   C. sister   D. brother

E. husband   F. wife   G. son   H. daughter

1. brother _____   5. _____

2. _____   6. _____

3. _____   7. _____

4. _____   8. _____

2. Complete the Sentences

1. Who is ___he__ ?   _____ is my brother.

2. Who is _____ ?   _____ is my mother.

3. Who _____ they?   _____ are my children.

4. Who _____ your teacher?   _____ teacher is _____.

3. Write the Male and Female Family Words

Female	Male
1. mother	1.
2.	2.
3.	3.
4.	4.

Answer Key 1 John 3:1: See how much the Father has loved us! His love is so great that we are called God's children.

4. Write Sentences about your Family

1. _____

2. _____

3. _____

UNIT 2 – THE COMMUNITY
LESSON 1 – LOCATIONS OF PLACES

drug store

super market

on the corner of

hospital

mall

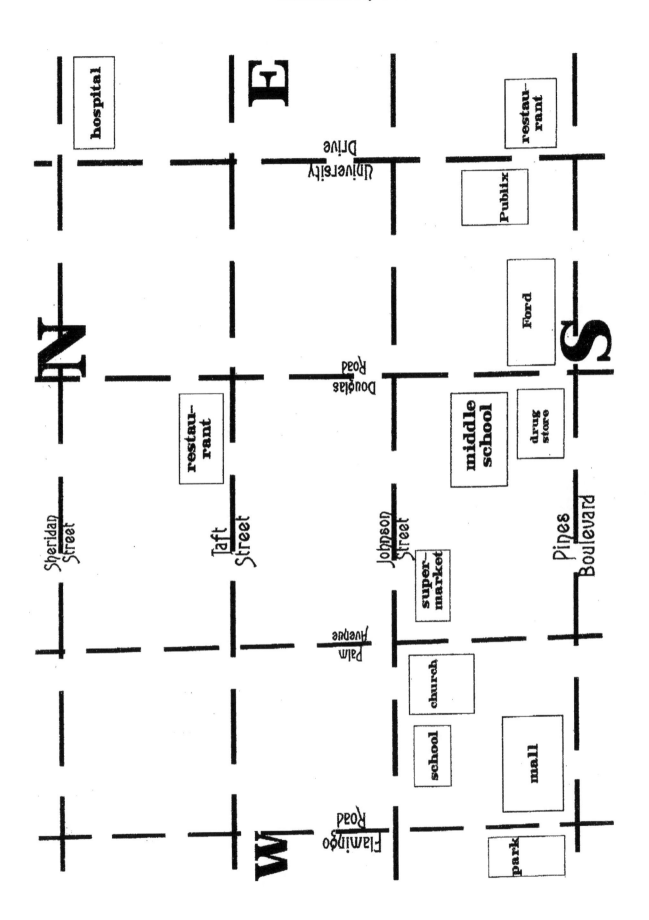

Time to Speak

To Do First: Repeat the conversation after the instructor.

1.A. Excuse me. Where's **the mall?**
   1.B. **Pembroke Lakes Mall** is **on Pines Boulevard.**
2.A. **On Pines Boulevard?**
   2.B. Yes. **It's on the corner of Pines Boulevard and Flamingo Road.**
3.A. Thanks.

To Do Second: Speak with a partner. Change the underlined words in the conversation for the Substitutions in No. 1-3 below.

Substitution No. 1.
1.A. Excuse me. Where's the **drug store**?
   1.B. **Walgreens Drug Store is on Douglas Road**.
2.A. On **Douglas Road**?
   2.B. Yes. It's on the corner of **Douglas Road** and **Pines Boulevard**.
3.A. Thanks.

Substitution No. 2.
1.A. Excuse me. Where's the **hospital**?
   1.B. **Memorial Hospital Pembroke Pines is on Sheridan Street.**
2.A. On **Sheridan Street**?
   2.B. Yes. It's on the corner of **Sheridan Street** and **University Drive**.
3.A. Thanks.

Substitution No. 3.
1.A. Excuse me. Where's the **supermarket?**
   1.B. **Winn Dixie Supermarket is on Palm Avenue**.
2.A. On **Palm Avenue**?
   2.B. It's on the corner of **Palm Avenue** and **Johnson Street**.
3.A. Thanks.

To Do Third: Change partners and do Substitutions 1-3 again.

~~*Practice Perfect Pronunciation*~~

In the question 'Where Is…' speakers contract the two words 'where is' into one word, the Contraction, WHERE'S. An apostrophe (') is used to show were letters have been dropped from the contraction. Practice pronouncing the contraction after the instructor.

Grammar Foundation

Prepositions of Location

Prepositions of Location are used to show the relationship of two objects to each other. Some common Prepositions of Location are: in, at, under, above, on, next to, between, across from, on the corner of. Here's the structure:

To Do First: Repeat each statement after the instructor.

Noun	+ Be +	Preposition +	Noun
The hospital	is	on	Sheridan Street.
The bank	is	next to	the post office.
The church	is	across from	the supermarket.
The sofa	is	in	the living room.
The book	is	on	the table.
My money	is	in	my purse.
The drug store is		on the corner of Douglas Road and Pines Boulevard.	

To Do Second:
The instructor will place a book somewhere, for example, on the table.
Students make a statement about the book with a Preposition of Location, for example, "The book is on the table."

To Do Third:
1. Work with a partner. Use your book.
2. Student 1 places the book somewhere, for example, on the table.
3. Student 2 will make a statement about the book with the correct Preposition of Location, for example, "The book is on the table."
4. Student 2 places the book somewhere.
5. Student 1 makes a statement with the Preposition of Location.

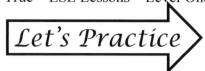

Let's Practice

1. Read a Map
To Do: Open your book to your map. Follow the instructor's directions.

2. Map Statements Listening
To Do:

1. Open your book to your map.
2. Number a piece of paper 1-6.
3. The instructor will make a statement about the map. For example: The drug store is on the corner of Pines Boulevard and Douglas Road.
4. Look at your map. If the statement is correct, write 'True' on your paper. If the statement is NOT correct, write 'False' on your paper.

3. Play Beat the Cat

1. This game is like the TV show Wheel of Fortune. The instructor will put a puzzle on the board.
2. Students take turns guessing consonants.
3. If the consonant is in the puzzle, the instructor will write it on the line. If the consonant is NOT in the puzzle, the instructor will draw part of a cat.
4. Continue until only vowels are left in the puzzle.

4. Map Reading
To Do:

1. Work with a partner. Use your map.
2. Student 1 asks a question about the map, for example: 'Where's the mall?'
3. Student 2 answers the question, for example: 'The mall is on the corner of Pines Boulevard and Flamingo Road.'
4. Student 2 asks a question about the map.
5. Student 1 answers the question.

5. Listening for Information
To Do:

1. The instructor will write a question on the board.
2. The instructor will read a passage. Listen for the answer to the question.

Jesus said to his disciples: "The Kingdom of God does not come in a way that you can see it. No one will say, 'Look, here it is!' or, "There it is!'; because the Kingdom of God is within you."

Review Exercises

1. Hidden Word Puzzle

To Do:

Circle the words in the puzzle.

church   drug store   hospital   supermarket   school   mall

```
Q  W  E  L  R  P  A  R  K  T  R  J  K  L  N  M  E  W  B  C  X
I  J  H  X  N  M  K  L  P  O  I  U  S  C  H  O  O  L  K  H  Y
F  D  S  A  J  H  O  S  P  I  T  A  L  E  Q  W  R  N  M  C  W
C  C  H  U  R  C  H  H  H  I  O  U  N  L  E  W  C  H  K  W  M
J  I  W  A  C  R  O  S  S  F  R  O  M  K  L  J  N  B  D  G  O
K  J  E  O  I  N  K  O  I  U  E  U  O  O  J  M  A  L  L  K  D
J  K  I  J  E  R  T  W  Q  S  D  F  N  E  X  T  T  O  J  W  A
K  N  B  D  R  U  G  S  T  O  R  E  N  D  S  S  D  G  E  X  Z
N  K  L  S  U  P  E  R  M  A  R  K  E  T  H  N  B  V  G  D  J
```

2. Scrambled Spelling

To Do:

Unscramble the words. Spell the street names correctly. Write the names on the lines.

1. eniiurtvsy   rvdie   *University Drive* _____

2. hiadesrn   tetsre   _____

3. alpm   uvaene   _____

4. lmanoifg   ador   _____

5. iesnp   uoblvread   _____

6. ojnhosn   tertse   _____

UNIT 2 – THE COMMUNITY
LESSON 2 – EMERGENCIES

For emergencies call 911

THE POLICE

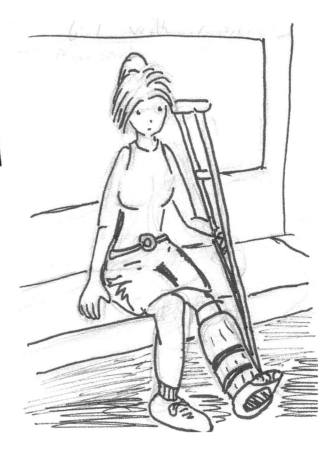

my mother broke her leg

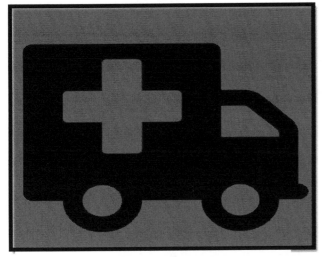

ambulance

there's a burglar
in my house

my house is on fire

Time to Speak

Calling 911 Emergency!

1.A.   911. Is this an emergency?

   1.B.   Yes! **My mother broke her leg**.

2.A.   **The ambulance is** coming. What's your name?

   2.B.   **Kathy Johnson**.

3A.   What's your address?

   3.B.   **50 Madrid Lane, Davie**

4.A.   What's your phone number?

   4.B.   **954.274.3105.**

5.A.   **The ambulance is** coming.

   5.B.   Thank you.

> *To Do First:*
>
> Repeat the conversation after the instructor.
>
> *To Do Second:*
>
> Speak with a partner. Change the underlined words in the conversation for the Substitutions.

Substitution No. 1

1.A.   911. Is this an emergency?

   1.B.   **There's a burglar in my house**!

2.A.   **The police** are coming. What's your name?

   2.B.   **Robin Francois.**

3.A.   What's your address?

   3.B.   **15427 N.W. 13 Street, Pembroke Pines.**

4.A.   What's your phone number?

   4.B.   **954.430.2387**.

5.A.   The police are coming.

   5.B.   Thank you.

Substitution No. 2

1.A.   911. Is this an emergency?

   1.B.   **There's a fire in my house**!

2.A.   **The fire department** is coming. What's your name?

   2.B.   **Juan Diaz**.

3.A.   What's your address?

   3.B.   **5140 S.W. 90 Avenue, Cooper City**.

4.A.   What's your phone number?

   4.B.   **954.436.9289**.

5.A.   **The fire department** is coming.

   5.B.   Thank you.

~~ *Practicing Perfect Pronunciation* ~~

Pronouncing Phone Numbers

English speakers pronounce phone numbers as follows:

954   274   31   05

This pronunciation is easy to understand because English speakers are expecting to hear phone numbers pronounced in this way.

To Do:

Repeat each phone number after the instructor. Use the pronunciation pattern above.

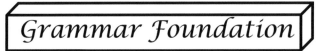
Grammar Foundation

Present Progressive Tense

Also known as Present Continuous Tense, we use the Present Progressive Tense to describe action that is happening at the present moment. It is continuous action. It is action that is happening while the speaker is speaking. Here's the grammar structure:

To Do: Repeat the sentences after the instructor.

Affirmative Statements

Subject + Be Verb + Main Verb + 'Ing Ending

Singular Forms

I	am	call	ing	911.
You	are	talk	ing	to the police.
He	is	send	ing	an ambulance.
She	is	tak	ing	a shower.
The house is		burn	ing.	

Plural Forms

We	are	do	ing	exercise.
We	are	study	ing.	
They	are	read	ing	their books.

Let's Practice ⟩

1. Play 911 Operator Concentration

1. Work with a partner or work with the whole class.

2. In the Concentration board are 8 cards. Four cards have 911 operator questions and 4 cards have answers.

3. Student 1 chooses 2 cards from the Concentration board and reads them to the class. For example: a question and the correct answer. If the 2 cards match – they are removed from the board and Student 1 receives one point.

4. Student 2 chooses 2 cards and reads them to the class. If these 2 cards do NOT match – Student 2 puts these cards back into the board.

5. Continue until all cards are matched and removed from the board.

2. Dictation – Addresses and Phone Numbers

The instructor will dictate some addresses and phone numbers. Write them below.

Addresses   Phone Numbers

1. _____

2. _____

3. _____

3. Emergency Role Play

Work with a partner. Student 1 is the 911 Operator. Student 2 is the caller with the emergency.

1. You saw two cars in an accident on I-95. A woman is hurt. Call 911.

2. Your neighbor is not home. Someone is breaking into his window.

3. Your husband fell off the ladder and he can't move. Call 911.

4. Play Beat the Cat

1. This game is like the TV show Wheel of Fortune. The instructor will put a puzzle on the board.

2. Students take turns guessing consonants.

3. If the consonant is in the puzzle, the instructor will write it on the line. If the consonant is NOT in the puzzle, the instructor will draw part of a cat.

4. Continue until only vowels are left in the puzzle.

Review Exercises

1. Complete the Conversation. Circle the Correct Word

1.A.   911. Is this an emergency / address?

   1.B.   Yes! My daughter broke / drank her arm.

2.A.   An _ambulance / fire department_ is coming. What's your _address / name_ ?

   2.A.   Kathy Smith.

3.A.   What's your   phone number / address?

   3.A.   11734 S.W. 55 Street, Cooper City.

4.A.   What's your name / phone number?

   4.B.   954.434.1101.

2. Write Answers to the Questions

1. Is this an emergency? Yes! _____

2. What's your name?   _____

3. What's your address?   _____

4. What's your phone number?   _____

3. Spell the Words Correctly

1. s d a e d r s   <u>A D D R E S S   </u>

2. p o e h n   m u n e b r   <u>   </u>

3. n g e e m c e y r   <u>   </u>

4. Complete the Sentences. Use the Present Progressive Tense and the Verbs in Parentheses

Example: (walk) John <u>*is walking*</u> to work right now.

1. (send) The 911 Operator _____ an ambulance now.

2. (call) The woman _____ 911 Emergency.

3. (watch) I _____ TV now.

4. (drink) They _____ Coca Cola now.

5. (send) The 911 Operator _____ the police.

6. (tell) The man _____ the 911 Operator his address.

7. (call) My mother and father _____ the 911 Operator.

8. (send) The 911 Operator _____ an ambulance.

9. (put) The firemen _____ out the fire.

10. (take) The burglar _____ my neighbor's TV.

UNIT 3 – LET'S EAT
LESSON 1 - SUPERMARKET DEPARTMENTS

Meat Department

Grocery Department

Bakery Department

Dairy Department

Produce Department

ground beef

orange

cupcake

peanut butter

turkey

milk

tomatoes

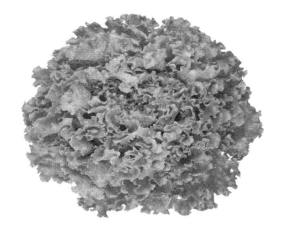

lettuce

cheese cake

butter

potatoes

paper towels

To Do First: Repeat the conversation after the instructor.

Shopping in the Supermarket

1.A.   What's on the shopping list today?

   1.B.   We need **milk and butter.**

2.A. They're in the **Dairy Department.**

   2.B.   We also need **ground beef and turkey.**

3.A.   They're in the **Meat Department.**

   3.B.   Good. We'll finish shopping quickly.

To Do Second: Speak with a partner. Change the <u>underlined words</u> in the conversation for the Substitutions in No. 1 and No. 2. below.

Substitution No. 1

   1.B.   oranges and potatoes

2.A.   Produce Department

   2.B.   paper towels and peanut butter

3.A.   Grocery Department

Substitution No. 2

   1.B.   lettuce and tomatoes

2.A.   Produce Department

   2.B.   cheesecake and cupcakes

3.A.   Bakery Department

To Do Third: Change partners and repeat Substitutions No. 1 and No. 2 again.

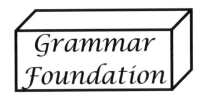

Grammar Foundation

Contractions

English speakers use Contractions which are two words put together to form another shorter word. Some letters are left out of one of the words and an apostrophe ['] marks the place where the letters are left out.

To Do First: Repeat each contraction after the instructor.

Subject + Will = Contraction

I	will	I'll
you	will	you'll
he	will	he'll
she	will	she'll
it	will	it'll
we	will	we'll
they	will	they'll

Subject + Be = Contraction

I	am	I'm
you	are	you're
he	is	he's
she	is	she's
it	is	it's
we	are	we're
they	are	they-re

To Do Second:
1. The instructor will say the two words, for example, "I am".
2. The instructor will throw a ball to a student.
3. The student catches the ball.
4. The student says the contraction, for example, "I'm".
5. The student throws the ball to the instructor.

To Do Third:
1. Work with a partner.
2. Student 1 says the two words.
3. Student 2 says the Contraction.

4. Student 2 says the 2 words.
5. Student 1 says the Contraction.

To Do Fourth:
1. Work with a partner.
2. Take turns saying sentences with Contractions and the Vocabulary words.
3. Say your sentences for the class.

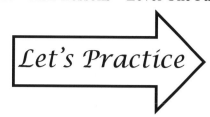

Let's Practice

1. Check Your Senses

To Do:

1. Smell each cup. Write what you think is inside.
2. Feel inside each bag. Write what you think is inside.

Cup 1 _____   Bag 1 _____

Cup 2 _____   Bag 2 _____

Cup 3 _____   Bag 3 _____

Cup 4 _____   Bag 4 _____

Cup 5 _____   Bag 5 _____

Cup 6 _____   Bag 6 _____

2. Search the Supermarket

To Do:

1. Draw a picture of one of the food words on a piece of paper, for example, draw an orange.
2. Draw two more pictures of different foods. Give your pictures to the instructor.

3. Supermarket Shopping

To Do:

1. On a piece of paper, write 5 of the food words.
2. Give your paper to the instructor.

4. Food Vocabulary Expansion

To Do:

1. Work with a small group. The instructor will give your group one of the supermarket departments, for example, the Meat Department.
2. With your group, write a list of foods you can find in your department. You can use your dictionary or your phone or tablet.
3. Share your list with the class.

5. What Do You Like?

To Do:

1. Talk with a small group.
2. Tell your group which foods you like to eat. Which foods do you not like to eat. What is your favorite food?

6. Practice English Rhythm

Jesus taught his disciples to pray to God and ask Him to give them food every day. Here's what Jesus told his disciples to pray:

Give us today our daily bread.

To Do:

Repeat the sentence after the instructor 7 times.

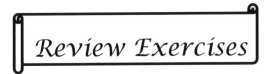
Review Exercises

1. Alphabetize

To Do:

Put the food words into alphabetical (A-Z) order.

milk	butter	ground beef	turkey	oranges	potatoes
tomatoes	lettuce	peanut butter	cheesecake	cup cakes	paper towels

_____butter, cheesecake_____

_____

_____

_____

_____

_____

2. Categorize

To Do: Put the food words into the Supermarket Departments.

Dairy	Meat	Produce	Grocery	Bakery
Butter				cheesecake

3. At Home

To Do:

Look in your kitchen. Write a list of 10 foods you have. Bring your list to the next class.

4. Matching

To Do:

Match the Full Form with the Contraction. Write the letter on the line by the Full Form.

	Full Form	Contraction
d.	I will	a. you're
	you will	b. she's
	he will	c. we're
	she will	d. I'll
	it will	e. he'll
	we will	f. it'll
	they will	g. they'll
	I am	h. he's
	you are	i. it's
	he is	j. they're
	she is	k. you'll
	it is	l. she'll
	we are	m. we'll
	they are	n. I'm

UNIT 3 – LET'S EAT
LESSON 2 – FOOD PACKAGING AND MEASUREMENTS

refrigerator

freezer

kitchen cabinet

a carton of juice

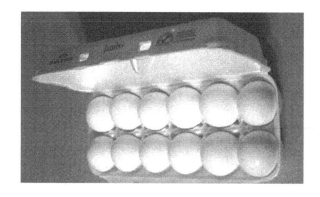

a dozen eggs

a box of crackers

a can of soup

a gallon of ice cream

a package of meat

Time to Speak

Is There Any More Juice?

To Do First: Repeat the conversation after the instructor.

1.A.   **Is there** any more **juice** in the **refrigerator**?
   1.B.   No, there **isn't**. We need to buy some more.
2.A.   What else do we need at the supermarket?
   2.B.   We need **a dozen eggs**.
3.A.   I'll make a list. O.K. that's **a carton of juice** and **a dozen eggs**.

To Do Second: Speak with a partner. Change the underlined words in the conversation for the Substitutions in No. 1-2 below.

Substitution No. 1

1.A.   **Are there** any more **crackers** in the **cabinet**?
   1.B.   No, there **aren't**.
2.A.   What else do we need at the supermarket?
   2.B.   We need **a can of soup**.
3.A.   I'll make a list. O.K. that's **a box of crackers** and **a can of soup**.

Substitution No. 2

1.A.   **Is there** any more **meat** in the **freezer**?
   1.B.   No, there **isn't**. We need to buy some more.
2.A.   What else do we need at the supermarket?
   2.B.   We need **a gallon of ice cream**.
3.A.   I'll make a list. O.K. that's **a package of meat** and **a gallon of ice cream**.

Grammar Foundation

To Do First: Read the information about Count and Noncount Nouns.   Repeat the example statements after the instructor.

1. Count and Noncount Nouns

1. Count Nouns can be counted as individual items, for example: an apple, a carrot, the car. Count Nouns also have a plural form, for example: four apples, a pound of carrots, 20 cars. Use an Article in front of the Count Noun: A, An, The, Some or Any.

2. Noncount Nouns cannot be counted because they are very small pieces and cannot be counted, for example: sugar, rice. Noncount Nouns can also be liquids such as water or milk. Noncount Nouns do not have a plural form. Use Some or Any in front of Noncount Nouns.

3. Noncount Nouns can be counted when they are inside of packages, but you are counting the package, which is a Count Noun, for example: 2 gallons of milk, 6 cartons of juice, 4 bags of rice.

To Do Second: Read the information about making statements and questions with THERE. Repeat the example statements after the instructor.

2. There is; There are; There isn't; There aren't

1. Use THERE IS… for Affirmative Statements with Singular Count Nouns and Noncount Nouns. For example:
   - There is an apple on the table.   [singular count]
   - There is some juice in the refrigerator.   [noncount]

2. Use THERE ARE … for Affirmative Statements with Plural Count Nouns.
   - There are some cookies in the cabinet. [plural count]
   - There are some cars in the parking lot.   [plural count]

3. Use IS THERE … ? for Questions with Singular Count Nouns and Noncount Nouns. For example:
   - Is there an apple on the table?   [singular count]   Yes, there is.
   - Is there any ice cream in the freezer?   [noncount]   No, there isn't.

4. Use ARE THERE … ? for Questions with Plural Count Nouns. For example:
   - Are there any cookies in the cabinet? [plural count]   Yes, there are.
   - Are there any apples on the table?   [plural count]   No, there aren't.

43

To Do Third: Read the information about using Some and Any with Count and Noncount Nouns. Repeat the example statements after the instructor.

3. Some and Any

1. Use SOME to make Affirmative Statements and ask Questions with Plural Count Nouns and Noncount Nouns. For example:
    *   I have some apples.   [plural count noun]
    *   We have some video games.   [plural count noun]
    *   He has some juice.   [noncount noun]
    *   They have some ice cream.   [noncount noun]
2. Use ANY to make Negative Statements and ask Questions with both Count and Noncount Nouns. For example:
    *   He doesn't have any apples.   [plural count]   Does he have any apples?
    *   He doesn't have any juice.   [noncount] Does he have any juice?
    *   We don't have any video games.   [plural count]   Do we have any video games?
    *   They don't have any ice cream. [noncount] Do they have any ice cream?

~~ Practicing Perfect Pronunciation ~~

I'm Going to the Store to Buy Some Eggs – Add On Game
1. The Instructor begins by saying, "I'm going to the store to buy some eggs."
2. Student 1 repeats the statement, "I'm going to the store to buy some eggs," and adds another item to the shopping list, for example: "I'm going to the store to buy some eggs and a carton of juice."
3. Student 2 repeats everything and adds another item.
4. Continue around the room until all have added something to the shopping list.

Let's Practice

1. Dictation
1. The instructor will put the food words on the board.
2. The instructor will dictate some measurements, for example: a box of...
3. Students write the measurements.
4. Students complete the sentences with the food words from the board.
5. Students read their sentences to the class.

2. There's a Carton of Juice in the Refrigerator

1. The instructor will draw a refrigerator, freezer, and kitchen cabinet on the board.
2. Each student receives some cards with food words.
3. Students place their food cards into the correct place: refrigerator, freezer, or kitchen cabinet.
4. Students make statements about the food, for example: 'There is a carton of juice in the refrigerator.'

3. Shopping List

1. Students work in groups of three.
2. Each group chooses one student to be the 'reader'.
3. The other 2 students will be 'writers'.
4. The instructor will put a shopping list outside the room on the wall.
5. The readers can go out to read the list, then come back and tell the writers what is on the list. Readers can go in and out as many times as they want. Writers can NOT go out of the room.
6. Groups read their shopping list to the class.
7. To win, a group must be first finished AND correct. Good Luck!

4. Twenty Questions

1. The instructor asks the class to think about one of the food words.
2. The instructor leaves the room while the class decides which food word to think about.
3. The instructor comes back into the room.
4. The class says, "We're thinking of a food."
5. For example, the class is thinking about ice cream.
6. The instructor asks questions that can be answered with YES or NO to discover which food the class is thinking about.
7. For example, the instructor may ask:
- "Is this food in a package?" The class says, "No."
- "Is this food cold?"   The class says, "Yes."
- "Is this food for breakfast?" The class says, "No."
- "Is this food in the refrigerator?   "   "   "No."
- "Is this food in the freezer?"   "   "   "Yes."
- "Is this food ice cream?"   "   "   "Yes!!!"

5. Scrambled Sentence

1. Students make 2 groups.
2. The instructor will give each group a set of cards with the words of a sentence.

3. Students work in their groups to put the sentence into correct order.

4. Groups read their sentence to the class.

Review Exercises

1. Writing

At home, look at the food in your kitchen cabinet, refrigerator, or freezer. What are your favorite foods? Write a paragraph of 3-4 sentences about your favorite foods.

In my kitchen I have some _____

_____

_____

_____

_____

2. Shopping List

Complete the Shopping List.

1. A _____ of ice cream

2. A _____ of meat

3. A _____ of soup

4. A _____ eggs

5. A _____ of juice

6. A _____ of crackers

3. What's in Your Kitchen?

Look in your kitchen cabinet, refrigerator, and freezer. Write foods that you have in the different packages.

1. A box   CRACKERS, COOKIES, PASTA, ZIP LOCK BAGS _____

_____

_____

_____

2. A can _____

_____

_____

_____

3. A carton _____

_____

_____

_____

4. A package _____

_____

_____

_____

UNIT 4 - SHOPPING
LESSON 1 – CLOTHING SIZE AND FIT

department store

colors

green   black   blue   red   brown

too tight

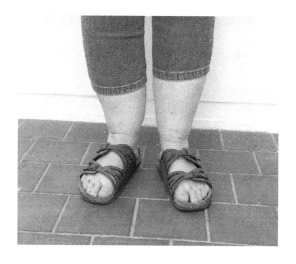

too short

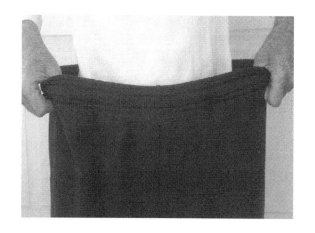

too large

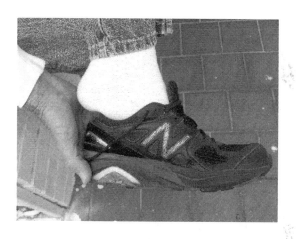

too small

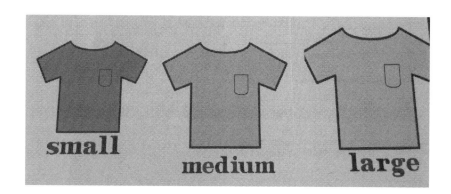

sizes

T-shirt

shirt

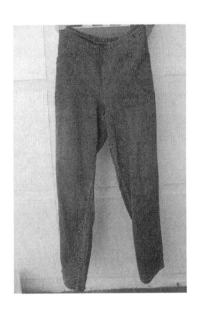

a pair of blue jeans

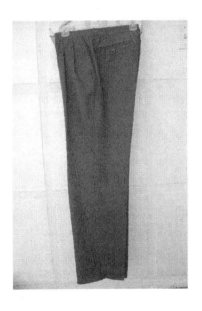

a pair of pants

blouse

Time to Speak

To Do First: Repeat the conversation after the instructor.

My Clothes are too Small

1.A.   My clothes are **too small**. Let's go shopping.
  1.B.   O.K.
2.A.   Here's a **medium brown blouse**. I'll try it on.
  2.B.   How does it fit?
3.A.   It fits good.

To Do Second: Speak with a partner. Change the underlined words in the conversation for the Substitutions in No. 1-4 below.

Substitution No. 1

1.A.   too tight
2.A.   small red T-shirt

Substitution No. 2

1.A.   too short
2.A.   large pair of blue jeans

Substitution No. 3

1.A.   too large
2.A.   medium pair of black pants

Substitution No. 4

1.A.   too large
2.A.   small green shirt

Grammar Foundation

Using Too

Too is used in front of Adjectives. It implies a negative result. For example:

The computer is too expensive.	Negative Result – We cannot buy it.
The pants are too big.	Negative Result – The pants don't fit.
The box is too heavy.	Negative Result – I can't pick it up.
The T-shirt is too dirty.	Negative Result – I can't wear it.

To Do First:

Repeat each sentence after the instructor.

To Do Second:

Circle the best result for the sentences.

1. My pants are too tight.
   A. I can wear them.
   B. I can't wear them.

2. The blouse is too expensive.
   A. I can't buy it.
   B. I can buy it with my credit card.

3. My son is too heavy.
   A. I can pick him up.
   B. I can't pick him up.

4. These shoes are too tight.
   A. I can't wear them.
   B. I can wear them tomorrow.

5. These jeans are too large.
   A. I have to return them to the store.
   B. I can wear them tonight.

~~ Practicing Perfect Pronunciation ~~

Can and Can't - Can is the ability to do something. Can't is the opposite – not able to do something.

To Do:

1. Repeat Can and Can't after the instructor.
2. Close your eyes and listen to the instructor. Raise your hand when the instructor says 'Can'. Don't raise your hand if the instructor says 'Can't'.

Practicing 'S' Sounds in Rhythm

To Do: Repeat after the instructor.

Suzy's Terrible Togs

Too short, too short, too short,   my jeans are t-o-o short.

Too tight, too tight, too tight,   my blouse is t-o-o tight.

Too small, too small, too small,   my shoes are t-o-o small.

Too large, too large, too large,   my pants are t-o-o large.

My jeans are so short

My blouse is so tight

My shoes are so small

My pants are so large

Too short, too tight, too small, too large.

Too short, too tight, too small, too large.

Too short, too tight, too small, too large.

T-o-o b-a-d for Suzy!!

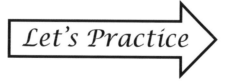

Let's Practice

1. Clothing Fit Listening Activity

To Do:

1. Listen to the conversations.
2. Circle the word in [brackets] that you hear.

1.A.   How does the [blouse - T-shirt] fit?
1.B.   I think it is too [small - short].

2.A. How does the [shirt - T-shirt] fit?

2.B. It is too [tight - short].

3.A. How do the [pants - shoes] fit?

3.B. They are too [tight – small].

4.A. How do the [jeans - pants] fit?

4.B. I think they are too [large - short].

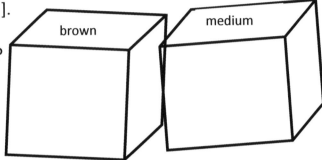

5.A. How does the [blouse - shirt] fit?

5.B. It is too [large - short].

2. Clothing Boxes

To Do:

1. Work in a small group.
2. The instructor will give you 4 boxes. Throw down the boxes on the table.
3. Make a sentence with the words on the top of the boxes. For example: 'The medium, brown blouse is too small.'
4. Share one of your sentences with the class.

3. Mystery Person

TO Do:

1. Work with a partner.
2. The instructor will think of one student.
3. Ask questions to the instructor to learn which student the instructor is thinking about. The instructor can only answer your question with YES or NO. For example, "Is this student wearing black pants?" Instructor will answer YES or NO.
4. When you think you know which student the instructor is thinking about, tell the instructor you want to guess.

4. Play Change the Chair

To Do:

1. Make a large circle of chairs with one less chair than students.
2. The student without a chair stands in the center.
3. The student in the center says, "Everyone wearing red, change chairs."
4. Everyone wearing red clothing must get up and move to another chair. The student in the center takes a chair.
5. The student without a chair stands in the center and gives the next direction.

5. Joseph's Coat – Add On Game

1. The instructor will draw a man with a striped coat on the board.
2. Student 1 comes to the board and colors one stripe with a red marker. Student 1 says, "Joseph had a coat of many colors. His coat was red."
3. Student 2 comes and colors another stripe blue. Student 2 repeats, "Joseph had a coat of many colors. His coat was red and blue." Repeat until all stripes are colored.

Review Exercises

1. Write Sentences

Write 5 sentences about the clothing your family is wearing, for example: My daughter is wearing a white shirt and a pair of blue jeans. Share your sentences in class.

1. _My daughter is wearing a white shirt and a pair of blue jeans._
2. _____
3. _____
4. _____
5. _____

2. Scrambled Sentences

Unscramble the sentences and put them into correct order. Use all the words.

1. my   is   a   and   pair   jeans   T-shirt   wearing
   of   a   blue   red   son   _My son is wearing_
   _____

2. pants   tight   black   too   my   are
   _____

3. pants   my   too   are   and   green   too   large
   short
   _____

4. pants   wearing   a   I   and   am   a   of   white
   black   pair   T-shirt
   _____

UNIT 5 - HOUSING
LESSON 1 – CHOOSING HOUSING

TYPES OF HOUSING

apartment

townhouse

house

mobile home

to move

for rent sign

above – bedroom

above right – bathroom

right – lease

To Do May 1

Lease is up

Move

To Do First: Repeat the conversation after the instructor.

It's Time to Move

1.A.   My lease is up. I have to move.
  1.B.   Oh, there's **an apartment** for rent next to me.
2.A.   How many bedrooms does it have?
  2.B.   It has **two** bedrooms.
3.A.   That's good. How much is the rent?
  3.B.   It's **$950** a month.
4.A.   O.K. Let's go see it.

To Do Second: Speak with a partner. Change the <u>underlined words</u> in the conversation for the Substitutions in No. 1-3 below.

Substitution No. 1
  1.B.   a house
  2.B.   three
  3.B. $1,200

Substitution No. 2

  1.B.   a mobile home
  2.B.   two
  3.B. $800

Substitution No. 3

  1.B.   a townhouse
  2.B.   three
  3.B. $1,150

Grammar Foundation

Using A Vs. An

1. 'A' and 'AN' are called Articles. They are used in front of Singular Nouns.
2. Use the article "A" before All Singular Nouns beginning with a consonant letter. For example: a house; a car; a mobile home; a newspaper; a townshouse.
3. Use the article "AN" before all Singular Nouns beginning with the vowel letters: "A, E, I, or O." For example:

   an apartment   an example   an ice cream cone   an oven
4. For Singular Nouns beginning with the vowel letter "U", use the article "AN" if the "U" sound is like the sound at the beginning of the words "uncle" or "ugly." For example:

   an understanding   an ugly house   an umbrella
5. Use the article "A" if the "U" sound is like the sound at the beginning of the words "university" or "usual". For example:

   a useless car   a unique experience

To Do First: Repeat the example words after the instructor.

To Do Second: Complete the sentences using the correct Article A or AN.

1. I have __an__ orange rug.
2. I live in _____ mobile home on the corner of Sheridan Street and Palm Avenue.
3. That townhouse is painted _____ ugly color.
4. There is _____ apartment building on the corner of University Drive and Pines Boulevard.
5. I live in _____ two bedroom apartment.
6. There is _____ university on the corner of Palm Avenue and Johnson Street.
7. _____ uncle of mine lives next door.
8. There is _____ ice cream cone in the dish on the dining table.

To Do Third: Share your responses with the class.

~~ Practicing Perfect Pronunciation ~~

The Statement Intonation Pattern is used for Statements – sentences that end with a period. The voice goes down on each sound unit and down at the end of the statement.

The easiest way to hear the sound units is by listening to your instructor. So, repeat each phrase after the instructor. Listen for the voice going down.

1. A two bedroom apartment, $950 a month.

2. A two bedroom mobile home, $800 a month.

3. A two bedroom mobile home, $750 a month.

4. A three bedroom house, $1,300 a month.

5. A three bedroom townhouse, $1,175 a month.

Listen again to the instructor read the sentences. Draw a line to show where the voice goes down. The instructor will demonstrate.

1. Dictation

The instructor will dictate some dollar amounts. Write the amount you hear below. For example, if you hear, "One hundred fifty dollars," you will write: $150.00.

1. _____   4. _____

2. _____   5. _____

3. _____   6. _____

2. Real Estate Ads Cloze Activity

Listen to the instructor read the ads. Write the missing words you hear on the lines.

Ad No. 1: Two ____bedroom____ apartment for rent, $1,325 a _____.   Call 954-_____.

Ad No. 2: Three bedroom house for _____, $_____ a month.   Call 954-432-9877.

Ad No. 3: _____ bedroom mobile home for rent, $700 a month.
Call _____ .

Ad No. 4: Four bedroom _____ for rent, three bathrooms, $1,800 a
_____ . Call _____ .

3. Choose Housing for Marie and Jean – Group Activity

Marie and Jean's lease is up. They have to move. Here's a list of some places they can choose.

1. Work with a group of 3 students.
2. Choose the best new home for Marie and Jean.
3. Tell the class which home you chose and what reasons you chose that home.

Housing	Rent	Neighborhood	Features
1. apartment	$900	Cooper City	2 bedrooms
2. mobile home	$950	Pembroke Pines	1 bedroom
3. house	$975	Weston	3 bedrooms
4. townhouse	$925	Hollywood	1 bedroom
5. house	$1,125	Pembroke Pines	4 bedrooms
6. mobile home	$800	Miramar	2 bedrooms

Which housing would you choose for Jean and Marie? _____

_____

Why? _____

4. Our Favorite House – Group Discussion

1. Work with a small group.
2. In 2 minutes, describe your house to the group. For example: I live in a house. It has 3 bedrooms, 2 bathrooms, and a garage for 2 cars. It has a large yard with trees. I like my house because it is large and it costs only $650 a month.

5. Play Beat the Cat

1. This game is like the TV show Wheel of Fortune. The instructor will put a puzzle on the board.
2. Students take turns guessing consonants.
3. If the consonant is in the puzzle, the instructor will write it on the line. If the consonant is NOT in the puzzle, the instructor will draw part of a cat.
4. Continue until only vowels are left in the puzzle.

1. Read Housing Ads

Read each real estate ad. Answer the questions about the ads.

Number 1

Two bedroom apartment
for rent, in Cooper
City, $1,300 a month.
Call 954.435.1355.

Number 2

Three bedroom house
for rent, in Pembroke
Pines, $1,550 a month,
Call 954.431.5220.

Number 3

Two bedroom mobile
home for rent, in
Hollywood, $775 a
month, parking for 3
cars. Call 954.983.8700.

1. How much is the rent for the mobile home?_____

2. Which ad has parking for 3 cars?   _____

3. Where is the apartment?   _____

4. How many bedrooms does the house have?   _____

5. How much is the rent for the house?_____

6. Which ad has the highest rent?   _____

7. Which ad has the lowest rent?   _____

8. Where is the house?   _____

UNIT 5 - HOUSING
LESSON 2 – MOVING IN

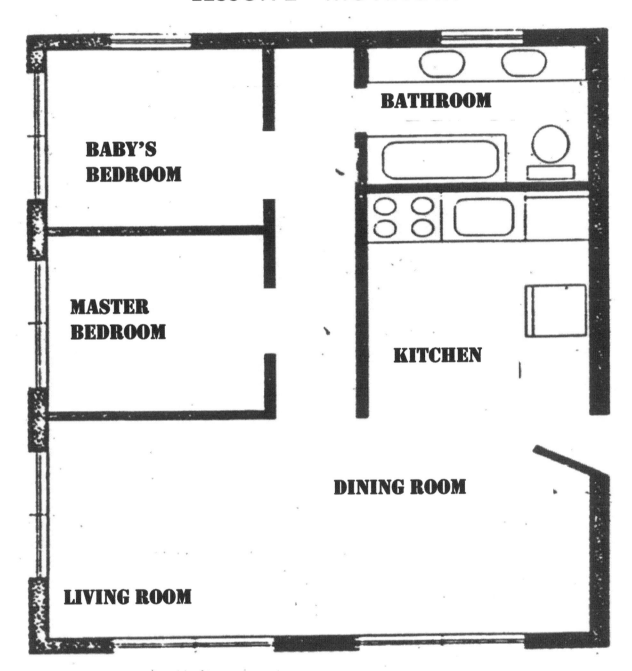

baby's room

living room

kitchen

master bedroom

bathroom

dining room

sofa

crib

chair

books

towels

table

To Do First: Repeat the conversation after the instructor.

Moving In

Speaker A: the moving company employee
Speaker B: the home owner

1.A.   Where do you want **this bed**?
   1.B.   **That bed** goes in the **master bedroom**.
2.A.   Where do you want **these chairs**?
   2.B.   **Those chairs** go in the **dining room**.

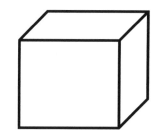

To Do Second: Speak with a partner. Change the <u>underlined words</u> in the conversation for the Substitutions No. 1-2 below.

Substitution No. 1
1.A.   Where do you want **this sofa**?
   1.B.   **That sofa** goes in the **living room**.
2.A.   Where do you want **these books**?
   2.B.   **Those books** go in the **baby's room**.

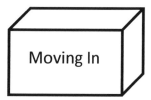

Moving In

Substitution No. 2
1.A.   Where do you want **this table**?
   1.B.   **That table** goes in the **kitchen**.
2.A.   Where do you want **these towels**?
   2.B.   **Those towels** go in the **bathroom.**

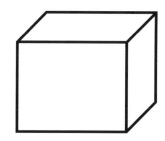

To Do Third: Partners present their conversations to the class.

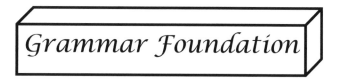

Grammar Foundation

To Do First: Read the information about Demonstratives. Repeat each demonstrative after the instructor.

Using DEMONSTRATIVES - THIS, THAT, THESE, THOSE

DEMONSTRATIVES are used with nouns to explain which noun we are speaking about. THIS and THAT are used with Singular Nouns while THESE and THOSE are used with Plural Nouns.

- THIS is used when the noun is in the speaker's possession or near to the speaker.
- THAT is used when the noun is not in the speaker's possession or not near to the speaker.
- THESE is used when the plural nouns are in the speaker's possession or near to the speaker.
- THOSE is used when the plural nouns are not in the speaker's possession or near to the speaker.

To Do Second:

1. The instructor will place the vocabulary words around the room.
2. The instructor will stand next to a word, for example, 'chair'. The instructor will say, "this chair."
3. The instructor will move across the room and point to the chair. The instructor will say, "that chair."
4. The instructor will repeat with all the Vocabulary words using This, That, These, or Those. Students repeat along with the instructor.

To Do Third:

1. Practice with a partner. Use your books and your pencils.
2. Student 1 picks up one book and says, "this book." Student 1 puts the book down on the other side of the table, points to the book and says, "that book."
3. Student 2 picks up two pencils and says, "these pencils." Student 2 puts the pencils down on the other side of the table, points to the pencils and says, "those pencils."
4. Continue until both partners have practiced all Demonstratives.

To Do Fourth:

1. Read the information about Where + Do.
2. Repeat the example sentences after the instructor.

Questions with WHERE + DO

WHERE + DO is used to ask about the location for something.

Where + Do/Does + Subject + Main Verb + Object

Where	do	you	want	this bed?
Where	do	you	want	these chairs?
Where	do	you and Tom	want	these desks?
Where	do	the students	want	these books?
Where	does	John	want	these towels?
Where	does	Marie	want	these dishes?
Where	does	your wife	want	this sofa?

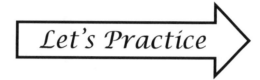

Let's Practice

1. Dictation

To Do: The instructor will say the name of a furniture word, for example, 'bed'. Write the word under the correct room. Write 'bed' under the Bedroom.

Bedroom	Living Room	Kitchen	Bathroom
Bed			

2. Furniture Bingo

To Do:

1. The instructor will give you a Furniture Bingo card and some candy. Use the candy for 'Bingo chips.'

2. The instructor will point to a picture of some furniture, for example, a table.

3. Students look for the word 'table' on their Bingo cards and place a Bingo chip.

4. When students get 3 Bingo chips in a row, shout "Bingo". The instructor will ask you what words you have.

3. Rearrange the Furniture – Listening Activity

To Do:

1. Tear a piece of paper into 7 small pieces.
2. Write the following furniture words one on each paper: crib, bed, chair, table, sofa, TV, books.
3. Open your book to the apartment floor plan.
4. The instructor will give a command, for example: "put the sofa in the living room." Students will place their 'sofa' paper into the living room.

4. Mover/Home Owner - Role Play

To Do:

1. The instructor will place room signs around the classroom. Work with a partner. Use the small furnitue papers from Rearrange the Furniture activity.
2. Student 1 is the Mover. Student 2 is the Home Owner.
3. The Mover asks the Home Owner, for example: "Where do you want this table?"
4. The Home Owner says, "Put that table in the dining room."
5. The Mover takes the table paper and puts it into the dining room.
6. Continue until all furniture has been placed in the room.
7. Change roles and repeat.

5. Scrambled Sentence

To Do:

1. Below you will see the words for a sentence.
2. Put the words into correct order. Write it on the line.
3. Read the sentence. It is from Hebrews 3:4 in the Bible.

can build / made everything / many people / houses, but only God

_____

_____

Review Exercises

Using This, That, These, and Those

To Do: Complete the conversation. Use this, that, these, or those.

1.A. Where do you want <u>this</u> bed?

   1.B. Put _____ bed in the master bedroom.

2.A. Where do you want _____ chairs?

   2.B. Put _____ chairs in the dining room.

3.A. Where do you want _____ TV?

   3.B. Put_____ TV in the living room.

4.A. Where do you want _____ curtains?

   4.B. Put _____ curtains in the kitchen.

5.A. Where do you want _____ towels?

   5.B. Put _____ towels in the bathroom.

6.A. Where do you want _____ books?

   6.B. Put _____ books in the living room.

7.A. Where do you want _____ crib?

   7.B. Put _____ crib in the baby's bedroom.

8.A. Where do you want _____ pictures?

   8.B. Put _____ pictures in the dining room.

9.A. Where do you want _____ TV?

   9.B. Put _____ TV in the master bedroom.

10.A. Where do you want _____ sofa?

   10.B. Put _____ sofa in the living room.

2. Write Sentences about your Furniture

To Do:

Write sentences about your furniture in your house. Use this, that, these, and those.
For example:

1. *I put that bed in my bedroom.* _____

2. _____

3. _____

4. _____

5. _____

3. Draw a Floor Plan of your House

To Do:

1. Draw a floor plan of the house or apartment where you live. Use the example floor plan in the book. Share your floor plan with the class

Unit 5 - Housing
LESSON 3 – CLEANING HOUSE

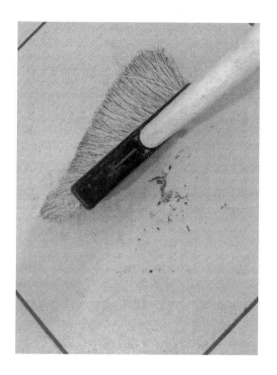

sweep the floor

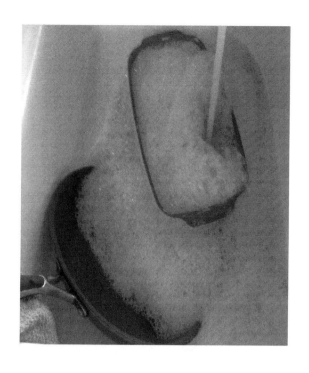

do the dishes

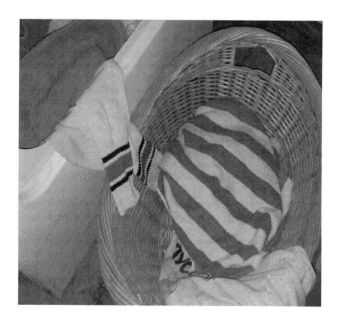

do the laundry

take out the trash

laundry detergent

dish detergent – under the sink

broom

trash bags

in the closet

in the cabinet

To Do First: Repeat the conversation after the instructor.

Cleaning House

Speaker A: Mother
Speaker B: Children

1.A.   It's time to clean the house. **Mary, wash the dishes.**
   1.B.   Where's the **dish detergent**?
2.A.   The **dish detergent** is **under the sink**.
   2.B.   O.K.
3.A.   **John, do the laundry.**
   3.B.   Where's the **laundry detergent**?
4.A.   The **laundry detergent** is **in the cabinet**.
   4.B.   O.K.

To Do Second: Speak with a partner. Change the underlined words in the conversation for the Substitutons in No. 1 below.

Substitution No. 1
1.A.   It's time to clean the house. **Hiromasa, sweep the floors**.
   1.B.   Where's the **broom?**
2.A.   The **broom is in the closet**.
   2.B.   O.K.
3.A.   **Megumi, take out the trash**.
   3.B.   Where're the **trash bags**?
4.A.   The **trash bags are in the cabinet**.
   4.B.   O.K.

To Do Third: Partners present their conversations for the class.

Grammar Foundation

To Do First: Read the information about Imperative Commands with the instructor.

To Do Second: Repeat the example sentences after the instructor.

1. Imperative Commands

The Imperative is used to give a command or an instruction. The sentence usually begins with the command. Examples of imperatives for this lesson include: wash, do, sweep, and take out.

Imperatives are used when you want to tell someone to do something such as commands, orders, instructions, or polite requests. In an Imperative sentence, use the base form of the verb. Imperatives are often used without a subject in the sentence. For example:

Stop!
Open the door.
Do the laundry.
Please take out the garbage.

The negative imperative uses 'Don't'.

Don't talk to me.
Don't wash the dishes.
Don't answer the phone.
Please don't do that.

When you want someone to do something with you, use 'Let's'.

Let's go to the park.
Let's sweep the floors..
Let's make a long distance phone call.

NOTE: Often an imperative is preceded by the person's name to whom the command or direction is given. For example: John, do the laundry.

To Do Third:

1. Speak with a partner.
2. Student 1 makes an Imperative Command, for example, 'stand up'.

3. Student 2 performs the action.
4. Student 2 makes an Imperative Command.
5. Student 1 performs the action.

2. Prepositions of Location

To Do First: Read the information about Prepositions of Location. Repeat the example sentences after the instructor.

Prepositions of Location are used to show the relationship of two objects to each other. Some common Prepositions of Location are: in, at, under, above, on, next to, between, across from, etc. Here's the structure:

Noun   + Be + Preposition + Noun

The dish soap	is	under	the sink.
The dryer	is	next to	the washing machine.
The church	is	across from	the supermarket.
The laundry	is	on	the table.
The trash bags	are	under	the sink.
The broom	is	in	the closet.
The dishes	are	in	the dish washer.
The laundry	is	in	the dryer.

To Do Second:
1. The instructor will place an object somewhere in the room, for example, the instructor places a book on the table.
2. Students respond with a statement about the book.
3. Use the correct preposition, for example: "The book is on the table".

To Do Third:
1. The instructor will place an object somewhere in the room, for example, the instructor places a book on the table.
2. The instructor will ask Student 1: "Where's the book?"
3. Student 1 answers: "The book is on the table."
4. The instructor moves the object to another place in the room.
5. Student 1 asks to Student 2: "Where's the book?"
6. Student 2 answers.
7. Continue until all students have asked and answered questions.

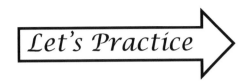

1. Verbs in the Bag

To Do:

1. Student 1 takes a card from the bag and performs the action without speaking.
2. For example, the card says: sweep the floor. Student 1 pantomimes sweeping the floor. The class guesses what action Student 1 is doing.

2. Cleaning Tasks and Products Mix & Match

1. The instructor will give each student a card. Half of the cards have cleaning tasks, for example: 'sweep the floor'. The other half of the cards will have the cleaning products or tools, for example: 'broom'.
2. Students walk around to find the match for their card.
3. Read matches to the class.

3. House Cleaning Survey

To Do:

Students talk to each other. Ask: Who does the house cleaning jobs in your family? Write the student's names under the cleaning jobs.

Name	Dishes	Laundry	Sweeping	Taking out Trash
Barbara	Barbara	Barbara	Bernie	Bernie

4. Every Week We Clean the House – Add On Game

1. Student 1 takes a cleaning job card from the bag, for example: 'sweep the floor.' Student 1 makes a sentence, "Every week we clean the house. I sweep the floor." Student 2 takes a card from the bag, for example: 'wash the dishes'.

2. Student 2 repeats Student 1's statement, then adds a statement, for example: "Every week we clean the house. HE sweeps the floor, and I wash the dishes."
3. Continue until all students have added a cleaning job.

5. The Lost Coin Pantomime

To Do First:

1. The class chooses one student to be the Reader.
2. The instructor will be the Actor.
3. The Reader reads the sentences. Stop at the end of each sentence so the instructor can perform the actions.

Reader	Instructor
1. A woman had 10 $1,000 dollar bills.	Woman counts her money out loud.
2. She loses 1 of the $1,000 dollar bills.	Woman counts again; only 9 bills.
3. What does she do?	Woman panics.
4. She turns on the light.	Woman turns on the light.
5. She sweeps her house.	Woman sweeps whole house.
6. She looks carefully everywhere.	Woman looks around whole room.
7. She finds the money!	Woman finds the lost money.
8. When she finds it, she calls her friends.	Woman calls friends on cell phone.
9. The woman says:	Woman shouts, "I'm happy! I have found my lost money!"

To Do Second: Listen to the instructor tell the meaning of the story.

Review Exercises

1. Writing

_To Do:_ Write 5 sentences about the house cleaning jobs you do each week.

Every week I do the laundry. _____

_____

_____

_____

_____

2. Mystery Word Search

To Do First:

1. Complete the sentences No. 1-10 below.
2. Write the answer from the sentences on the lines in the puzzle with one letter on each line.
3. When finished, a mystery word will appear inside the box.
4. Write the mystery word on the line.

1. My trash bags are in the _cabinet._

2. I _____ _____ every week.

3. I use a broom to _____ _____ _____.

4. I _____ _____ every day.

5. My dish detergent is under the _____.

6. I use _____ _____ to wash dishes.

7. My _____ is in the closet.

8. I use _____ _____ to wash clothes.

9. I use large black _____ _____.

10. My broom is in the _____.

To Do Second: Write the answers to the questions above on the lines below.

1.

        C A B I N E T

2.

3.

4.

5.

6.

7.

8.

9.

10.

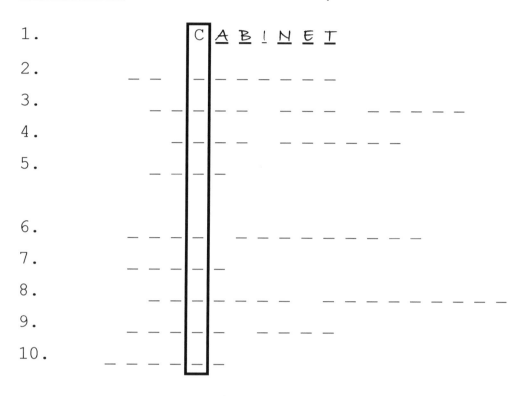

To Do Third: Write the mystery word inside the box on the line: _____.

Look how far you've come! Just a little more to go!

UNIT 6 - MEDICAL
LESSON 1 – THE BODY

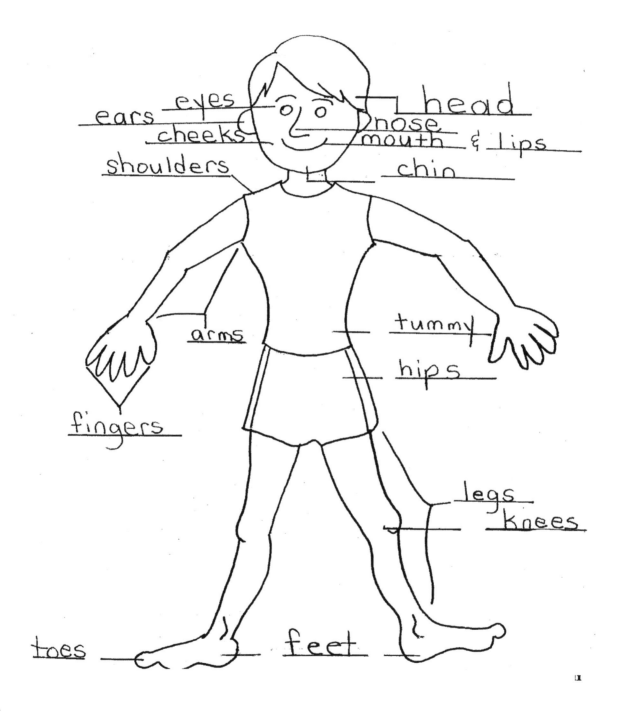

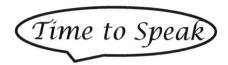

To Do First: Repeat the conversation after the instructor. Touch each of your body parts as you say them.

The Body

Speaker A - Parent
Speaker B - Child

1.A. Hi Johnny. What did you learn in school today?
   1.B. I learned the parts of the body.
2.A. Great! Show me the parts of the body.
   2.B. O.K. We learned them with a chant. Say it after me.
   My feet, my tummy, my arms, my chin.
3.A. My feet, my tummy, my arms, my chin.
   3.B. My legs, my lips, my hips, my cheeks.
4.A. My legs, my lips, my hips, my cheeks.
   4.B. My eyes, my ears, my mouth, my nose.
5.A. My eyes, my ears, my mouth, my nose.
   5.B. My head, my shoulders, my knees, my toes.
6.A. My head, my shoulders, my knees, my toes.
That's great, Johnny!

To Do Second: Spell the parts of the body after the instructor.

To Do Third: Work with a partner. Student 1 says one of the body parts. Student 2 touches his/her body part. Student 2 says one of the body parts. Student 1 touches his/her body part. Continue with all 16 parts of the body.

~~ Practicing Perfect Pronunciation ~~

Repeat each pair of words after the instructor:

eyes / ears   legs / lips   tummy / toes   chin / cheeks   hips / lips

Grammar Foundation

Possessive Adjectives

Use a Possessive Adjective before a Noun to show who the Noun belongs to. For example:

My mother.   Meaning: mother belongs to me. She is my mother.
My head.   Meaning: this head belongs to me. It is my head.
My house.   Meaning: this house belongs to me. I own this house. It's my house.
My children.   Meaning: the children belong to me. They're my children.
My father.   Meaning: father belongs to me. He's my father.

To Do First: Repeat the sentences after the instructor.

To Do Second: Repeat the Possessive Adjectives after the instructor.

Here's a chart of all the Possessive Adjectives:

Pronoun	Possessive Adjective	Pronoun	Possessive Adjective
I	my	it	its
you	your	we	our
she	her	you	your
he	his	they	their

To Do Third: Practice the Possessive Adjectives.
1. The instructor will write the Pronouns on the board.
2. The instructor will hold up a book and point to one of the Pronouns on the board.
3. Students will answer with the correct Possessive Adjective. For example, if the instructor points to the Pronoun 'I', students will answer with the Possessive Adjective 'my' book.

To Do Fourth: Complete the Possessive Adjective sentences below.

1. I am sick. __My__ tummy hurts.
2. John broke _____ arm yesterday.
3. My cat got _____ tail caught in the door.
4. Johnny put on _____ shoes.
5. My grandparents wear glasses. _____ eyes are bad.

6. Jane wears a hearing aid. _____ ears are bad.

7. Mom and Dad, here are _____ keys.

8. We are going to the dentist. We have to get _____ teeth cleaned.

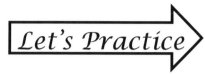

1. Simon Says

1. The instructor is 'Simon'.

2. Simon gives a command. Students respond. For example: "Simon says touch your nose." All students touch their noses.

3. If Simon gives a command and does NOT say "Simon says...", students should NOT perform the action. For example, the instructor says: "Touch your nose." Students should NOT perform the action.

4. If a student performs the action when the instructor does NOT say "Simon says...", that student is out and must sit down. The last student standing is the winner.

2. The Five Senses Concentration

To Do First: Learn the five senses: Taste, touch, hear, smell, see.
Repeat each sense after the instructor.

To Do Second: Match the five senses with the body part:

taste – mouth   touch – hands   hear – ears   smell – nose   see – eyes

Repeat each sense and body part after the instructor.

To Do Third: Practice the five senses and the body part.

1. The instructor will say one of the senses and throw a ball.

2. Student 1 catches the ball and says the body part. For example, the instructor says, "smell" and throws the ball. Student 1 catches the ball and says, "nose".

3. Student 1 throws the ball to the instructor.

To Do Fourth: Play Five Senses Concentration

1. Work with a partner or work with the whole class.

2. In the Concentration board are 10 cards. Five cards have senses and 5 cards have body parts.

3. Student 1 chooses 2 cards from the Concentration board and reads them to the class. For example: 'nose' and 'smell'. These 2 cards match – the body part and the correct sense. Cards are removed from the board and Student 1 receives one point.

4. Student 2 chooses 2 cards and reads them to the class. For example: 'eyes' and 'ears'. These 2 cards do NOT match – they are both body parts. Student 2 puts these cards back into the board.

5. Continue until all cards are matched and removed from the board.

3. Body Parts Line Up

   1. Work with a small group. The instructor will give each group a set of cards with the body parts.

   2. Group works together to put the cards into alphabetical order A-Z.

   3. Students read their cards to the class.

4. What Can The Body Do? - Group Brainstorm Activity

   1. Work with a partner. The instructor will give you one of the body parts, for example, the foot.

   2. Write a list of all the actions the foot can do, for example: walk, stand...

   3. Read your list to the class.

5. How God Created Man and Woman

Here's the story from the Scriptures about how God created man and woman. Later, you can read the whole story in Genesis 2:7-25.

To Do First: Listen to the instructor read the story. Follow along silently.

Genesis 2:7; 15; 18; 19A; 20B; 21-23:

   And the Lord God formed man from the dust of the ground and breathed into his nostrils the breath of life, and man became a living being. ... The Lord God took the man and put him in the Garden of Eden to work it and take care of it. . . . The Lord God said, "It is not good for the man to be alone. I will make a helper suitable for him." . . . Now the Lord God had formed out of the ground all the beasts of the field and all the birds of the air. . . . But for Adam no suitable helper was found. So the Lord God caused the man to fall into a deep sleep; and while he was sleeping, he took one of the man's ribs and closed up the place with flesh. Then the Lord God made a woman from the rib he had taken out of the man, and he brought her to the man. The man said, "This is now bone of my bones and flesh of my flesh; and she shall be called 'woman,' for she was taken out of man."

To Do Second: Close your books. Repeat each sentence after the instructor.

To Do Third:

   1. Use the instructor's pictures.

   2. Tell the story to your partner.

   3. Volunteers can tell the story to the class.

Review Exercises

1. Hidden Body Parts and Senses

Circle the body parts and senses in the puzzle.

tummy	arms	feet	chin	seeing	touch
legs	lips	hips	cheeks	hearing	body
eyes	ears	mouth	nose	taste	head
knees	toes	shoulders	smell		

```
A R M S N K L H F D S C H I N A K N Q I Y B O D Y N A S
A N I Y T O U C H N E W Q H N S B Q W E R T U M M Y W E
F N A E T Y F E E T G H J K O I U Y T S E E I N G W T E
N I Y N E W S M E L L E R T H E A D Y I O W Q E T O E S
Q W E R T Q W E R T T H E A D H I O E T R Q W H E H K E
N T R E Q Y I O P B V C S H O U L D E R S H Q T I Y I E
K K N E E S S B M A B J I Y K L E G S S N I Y Q E E B Q
N T H E A R I N G N H L I H H H I P S S Q W E R T T Y I
N L L I P S S N Y I Q W E R T N M N O B V Q W D A S D G
N K F D S C H E E K S N K L Q W D E R F T T G N K L P O
N O S E Q N H K N L E A R S N I Y E Y E S S E Y N O O S
Q W E R T Y N M O U T H B N M T A S T E B J K H G F D S
```

2. Complete the sentences

1. I use my ___mouth___ to taste and eat.

2. I use my _____ to smell.

3. I use my _____ to touch.

4. I use my_____ to see.

5. I use my _____ to hear.

3. Write the Story: How God Created Man and Woman

1. Below you will see the pictures for the story How God Created Man and Woman.
2. Write a sentence for each picture to tell the story.

1.

2.

3.

4. & 5.

6. & 7.

1.	
2.	
3.	
4.	
5.	
6.	
7.	

UNIT 6 - MEDICAL
LESSON 2 – PERSONAL HYGIENE

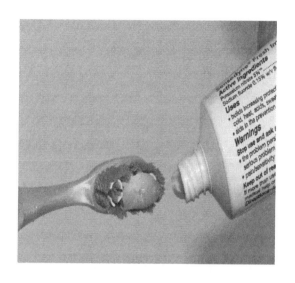

brush my teeth

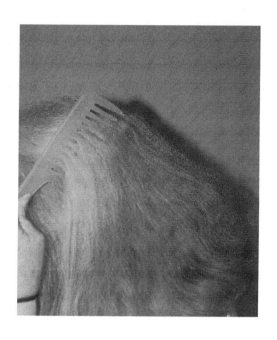

comb my hair

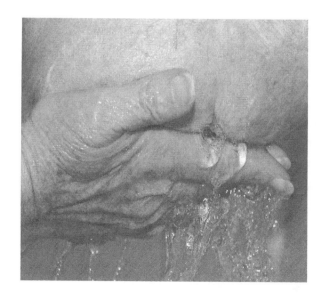

wash my face

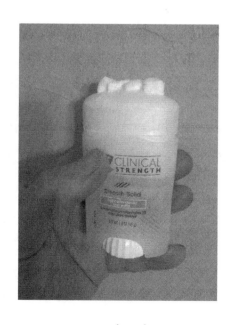

put on deodorant

take a shower

shampoo my hair

do exercises

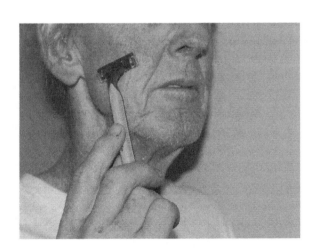

shave my face

My Daily Routine

To Do First: Repeat each sentence after the instructor.

1.A.   Every morning I **brush my teeth** and **wash my face.**
  1.B.   What does your **husband** do?
2.A.   **He shaves his face** and **takes a shower**.
  2.B.   What do you do in the evening?
3.A.   In the evening I **take a shower** and **shampoo my hair.**

To Do Second: Speak with a partner. Change the <u>underlined words</u> in the conversation for the Substitutions in No. 1-2 below.

Substitution No. 1
1.A.   **do exercise** and **comb my hair**
  1.B.   **brother**
2.A.   **washes his face** and **puts on deodorant**
3.A.   **comb my hair** and **put on deodorant**

Substitution No. 2
1.A.   **shampoo my hair** and **comb my hair**
  1.B.   **son**
2.A.   **He does exercise** and **brushes his teeth**
3.A.   **put on deodorant** and **brush my teeth**

To Do Third:
  1. Talk with your partner.
  2. Student 1 asks: "What do you do every morning?" Student 2 answers.
  3. Student 2 asks the question and Student 1 answers.
  4. Join with another pair of students. Student 1 tells the group what Student 2 does, for example: "My partner washes his face and brushes his teeth in the morning."
  5. Continue until all students have introduced their partners to the group.

Grammar Foundation

1. Simple Present Tense

Simple Present Tense is used to describe habits and usual activities done every day or regularly.

Use SIMPLE PRESENT TENSE in three ways:

(1) For habits and usual activities such as activities done every day or regularly.
   For example: I get up at 6:00 a.m. every day. I take a vacation every summer.
(2) For timeless facts or truth, generalizations.
   For example: The sun rises in the morning. The Spinach Salad recipe calls for spinach.
(3) For long term or permanent situations.
   For example: I live in Hollywood. My husbands works at the telephone company.

To Do First: Read the information about Simple Present Tense.

Affirmative Statements

Subject + Verb

I	brush	my teeth every day.
You	comb	your hair every morning.
He	shaves*	every night.
She	does*	exercises every day.
It	rains*	every June.
We	go	to church every Sunday.
They	eat	dinner every evening.

* Remember to put the final -s on the end of third person verbs

To Do Second: Repeat the example sentences after the instructor.

2. Present Progressive Tense

Present Progressive Tense is also known as Present Continuous Tense. We use the Present Progressive Tense to describe action that is happening at the present moment. It is continuous action. It is action that is happening while the speaker is speaking. Here's the grammar structure:

To Do First: Read the information about Present Progressive Tense.

Affirmative Statements

Subject + Be Verb + Main Verb + 'Ing Ending

Singular Forms

I	am	brushing	my teeth.
You	are	combing	your hair.
She	is	taking	a shower.
He	is	putting on	deodorant.

Plural Forms

We	are	doing	exercises.
You	are	watching	T.V.
They	are	shaving	their faces.

To Do Second: Repeat the example sentences after the instructor.

~~ *Practicing Perfect Pronunciation* ~~

Pronouncing -S Endings

1. Sounds are either Voiced or Voiceless For Voiced sounds, you use your voice box to vibrate the sound – for example, say: "shave, comb, shampoo." For Voiceless Sounds, your voice box does not vibrate – for example, say: "take, put."

2. Nouns ending in –S are pronounced with 3 different sounds. Feel your voice box. Put your hands on your throat. Say the Voiced words: "shave, comb, shampoo, do." Can you feel the voice box vibrating on the end of each word? Now pronounce some Voiceless words. Put your hand on your voice box and say these

words: "take, put." There's no vibration of the voice box. So, here's how to pronounce –S endings correctly:

- Voiced Ending Sounds Make a /z/ sound like a buzzing bee
- Voiceless Ending Sounds Make an /s/ sound like "shhh, be quiet"

3. The last group of –S ending words are pronounced with an extra syllable on the end of the word. Verbs that are spelled at the end with –SH; -CH; -SS; -X, for example: -SH – wash; CH – teach; SS – kiss; X – fix – add an extra syllable to the end of the word. The instructor will help you hear this pronunciation.

Let's Practice

1. Personal Hygiene Actions in the Bag Pantomime

To Do:

1. Student 1 takes a card with a personal hygiene action from the bag and performs the action without speaking.
2. The class guesses which action Student 1 is performing, for example: "You are brushing your teeth."
3. Student 2 takes a card and performs the action.
4. Continue until all students have performed a personal hygiene action.

2. Personal Hygiene Actions Concentration

To Do:

1. Work with a partner or work with the whole class. In the Concentration board are some cards. Half the cards have half of a personal hygiene action, for example: 'brush'. The other cards have the other half of the personal hygiene action for example: 'my teeth'. Student 1 chooses 2 cards from the Concentration board and reads them to the class. For example: "brush" and "my teeth". These 2 cards match – the complete personal hygiene action. Cards are removed from the board and Student 1 receives one point.
2. Student 2 chooses 2 cards and reads them to the class. For example: "brush" and "wash". These 2 cards do NOT match – they are both the first half of two different personal hygiene actions. Student 2 puts these cards back into the board.
3. *Continue until all cards are matched and removed from the board.*

3. Personal Hygiene Actions Survey

To Do:

1. Speak to your classmates.
2. Ask the question: "What personal hygiene actions do you do every day? "
3. Write your classmates' answers on your survey.

<u>Name</u>   <u>Question: What personal hygiene actions do you do every day?</u>

Barbara   *She washes her face and brushes her teeth.*

_____

_____

_____

_____

4. Play Beat the Cat

1. This game is like the TV show Wheel of Fortune. The instructor will put a puzzle on the board.
2. Students take turns guessing consonants.
3. If the consonant is in the puzzle, the instructor will write it on the line. If the consonant is NOT in the puzzle, the instructor will draw part of a cat.
4. Continue until only vowels are left in the puzzle.

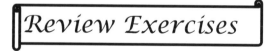

Review Exercises

1. Listing Personal Hygiene Actions

1. Read the personal hygiene actions.
2. Write each action a man does below under the column "Actions for Man", and each action a woman does unde the column "Actions for Woman".
3. Write actions that both man and woman do under the column "Actions for Man & Woman".
4. Add some of your own personal hygiene actions.

Personal Hygiene Actions

1. wash my face
2. comb my hair
3. brush my teeth
4. put on deodorant

5. shave my face
6. do exercise
7. shampoo my hair
8. take a shower

Actions for Man	Actions for Woman	Actions for Man & Woman
shave my face		*wash my face*

2. Simple Present Tense Vs. Present Progressive Tense

Complete the sentences with the correct form of the Verb in [brackets]. Use Simple Present Tense or Present Progressive Tense.

1. [brush] I __brush__ my teeth every morning.

2. [shave] My husband _____ his face right now.

3. [do] We _____ our exercises after work every day.

4. [take] My son _____ a shower now.

5. [put on] I always _____ deodorant in the morning.

6. [shampoo] I never _____ my hair at night.

7. [wash] Do you _____ your face every night?

8. [brush] Sorry I didn't answer the phone when you called. I was _____ my teeth.

Unit 6 – Medical
LESSON 3 – AT THE PHARMACY

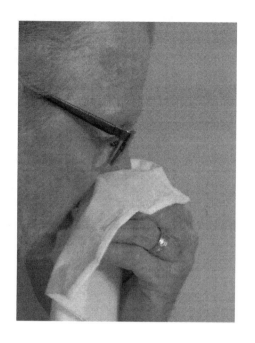

I have a cold

I have a headache

I have a sore throat

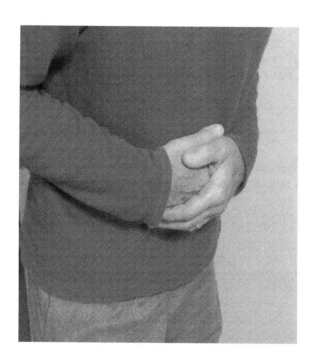

I have a stomachache

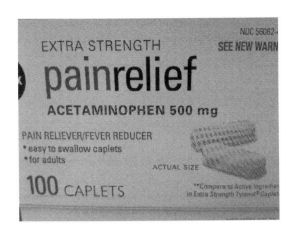

aspirin

cold medicine

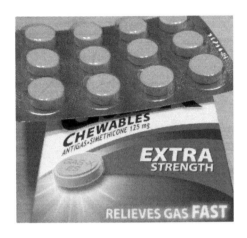

antacid tablets

throat lozenges

pharmacist

pharmacy

Time to Speak

To Do First: Repeat the conversation after the instructor.

At the Pharmacy

Speaker A: Customer/Patient   Speaker B: Pharmacist/Store Clerk

1.A.   Excuse me. I have **a headache**. What can I take?
   1.B. You can take **aspirin**.
2.A.   **Aspirin**?
   2.B.   Yes. **Aspirin** is on **Aisle 3**.
3.A.   Thank you.

To Do Second: Speak with a partner. Change the underlined words in the conversation for the Substitutions in No. 1-3 below.

Substitution No. 1
1.A.   Excuse me. I have **a cold**. What can I take?
   1.B.   You can take **cold medicine**.
2.A.   **Cold medicine**?
   2.B.   Yes. **Cold medicine is on Aisle 4.**
3.A.   Thank you.

Substitution No. 2
1.A.   Excuse me. I have **a sore throat**. What can I take?
   1.B.   You can take **throat lozenges**.
2.A.   **Throat lozenges?**
   2.B.   Yes. **Throat lozenges are on Aisle 2**.
3.A.   Thank you.

Substitution No. 3.
1.A.   Excuse me. I have **a stomachache**. What can I take?
   1.B.   You can take **antacid tablets**.
2.A.   **Antacid tablets**?
   2.B.   Yes. **Antacid tablets are on Aisle 6**.
3.A.   Thank you.

Grammar Foundation

Using Can and Can't; Could and Couldn't

We use CAN for ability and possibility. I am able to or it is possible for me to do something. For example:

- I can play the piano.
- You can take aspirin.
- They can take cough syrup.
- I can teach English.
- We can ask the pharmacist about cold medicine.
- John can't go to the party.

We use COULD for the past, for example:

- When I was young, I could run fast.
- Yesterday I could understand everything the teacher said.
- Last night I couldn't sleep.

Also, we use CAN YOU and COULD YOU to ask questions in the present or future tense. We use either CAN or COULD when we want to ask if something is possible to do, to make a polite request, or to ask permission to do something. For example:

Ask if something is possible to do

- Can I take aspirin for a headache?
- Could I take pain pills for a backache?
- Could he take antacid tablets for a stomachache?

Make a polite request

- Could you tell me how to get to Pines Baptist Church?
- Can I have chocolate, please?
- Can I speak to your brother?
- Could I borrow your book?

Ask permission to do something

- Could Johnny go to the beach with us?

To Do:
Repeat each example sentence after the instructor.

Using HAVE to Describe Physical Ailments

We use HAVE to describe a physical ailment which a person possesses.

Affirmative Statements

Subject + Have/Has + Object

I	have	a cold.
You	have	a sore throat.
She	has	a stomachache.
He	has	a backache.
We	have	headaches.
They	have	broken arms.

Let's Practice

1. Can & Can't Listening Activity

To Do:

Listen to the sentences. Circle the correct the word you hear [in brackets] to complete the sentence.

1. Juan [can / can't] find his throat lozenges.

2. Carol [can / can't] take cold medicine for her cold.

3. Ted [can't / can] take aspirin because he is allergic.

4. Where [can / can't] I find antacid tablets?

5. [Can / Cans] John take pain pills for a headache?

6. "When [can / cans] I take some aspirin?" Tommy asked.

7. [Can't / Can] Marie have a throat lozenge?

8. Ted [can't / can] take antacid tablets for his headache.

2. Medicine Mixer

To Do:

1. The instructor will give each student a card. Half of the cards have illnesses, for example: 'I have a cold'. The other half of the cards will have the medicines, for example: 'You can take cold medicine'.
2. Students walk around to find the match for their card.
3. Read matches to the class.

3. At the Pharmacy Role Play

To Do:

1. The instructor will set up a pharmacy inside the classroom.
2. Students work in pairs.
3. Student 1 is the customer and Student 2 is the pharmacist.
4. The customer asks the pharmacist for advice for a headache. The pharmacist tells what medicine to take and where to find it in the store.
5. Student 1 looks for the medicine on the shelves.
6. Change roles: Student 1 is the pharmacist and Student 2 the customer. Repeat until all students have been the customer and the pharmacist.

4. Play Beat the Cat

To Do First:

1. This game is like the TV show Wheel of Fortune. The instructor will put a puzzle on the board.
2. Students take turns guessing consonants.
3. If the consonant is in the puzzle, the instructor will write it on the line. If the consonant is NOT in the puzzle, the instructor will draw part of a cat.
4. Continue until only vowels are left in the puzzle.

To Do Second:

Listen to the instructor read the story.

To Do Third:

Read the story out loud with the instructor.

<u>Mark 8:22-25</u>

They came to Bethsaida, and some people brought a blind man and begged Jesus to touch him. He took the blind man by the hand and led him outside the village. When he had spit on the man's eyes and put his hands on him, Jesus asked, "Do you see anything?" He looked up and said, "I see people; they look like trees walking around." Once more Jesus put his hands on the man's eyes. Then his eyes were opened, his sight was restored, and he saw everything clearly.

Review Exercises

1. Answer the Questions with Complete Sentences

1. John has a cold. What can he take?

   He can take cold medicine.

2. My son has a stomachache. What can he take?

   _____

3. I have a sore throat. What can I take?

   _____

4. Mr. Jenkins has a headache. What can he take?

   _____

2. Match the Medicine with the Illness.

Write the letter of the illness on the line next to the medicine.

Medicines	**Illnesses**
1. _C._ antacid tablets	A. headache
2. _____ throat lozenges	B. cold
3. _____ aspirin	C. stomachache
4. _____ cold medicine	D. sore throat

ABOUT THE AUTHOR

Professor Barbara Kinney Black began her 25 year ESL teaching career as a volunteer in her church, University Baptist, in Coral Gables, Florida. She had taught for just 3 weeks when it became obvious to her that she could do something she loved for a career. She returned to university for a Master's of Science degree in T.E.S.O.L. Since that time she has taught ESL in a diversity of settings including:
Adult Education – Miami-Dade, Florida
College – Miami-Dade College, Miami, Florida - largest college in the U.S.A.
Seminary – New Orleans Theological Seminary - Miami Campus
China – Honghe University - sharing Western ESL teaching technique with Chinese English Teachers

Professor Black has authored ESL curriculum for a variety of applications including:
ESL for Florida Power and Light employees
ESL for employees of Global Mail Solutions
Co-authored <u>Teaching English Techniques & Practice</u> for Honghe University

Professor Black enjoys most her involvement since 1994 as a teacher/trainer for churches in Florida wishing to begin ESL ministries.
Professor Black has directed two ESL ministries in South Florida churches.

Above all, Professor Black delights in seeing her students succeed.